MRER
12/13

D1219679

Dear Parents,

Is your child a new reader? If yes, one good way to help your child build confidence and word recognition skills is by introducing word families.

The die-cuts at the bottoms of the pages draw attention to three different word families (letters show through each die-cut shape).

Once your child can read "**ice**", then he or she can focus on the beginning letters and sounds:

> **mice, rice, spice**

After the single words are learned, the pictures help your child read the words in phrases:

> **mice on ice**   **spice on rice**
> **mice eat spice**   **spice on ice and rice**

It's much easier to learn a group of words than to memorize them by sight one word at a time. A sight vocabulary is limited by the number of words that can be held in memory.

Recognizing words by families hugely increases the number of words that your child can know. It gives your child a way to sound out new words (reading specialists call these "word attack" skills), thereby increasing the likelihood he or she will feel successful.

Help your child with the 25 new words in this book by giving him or her multiple chances to read it until all the words are mastered.

Most important, have fun together!

Harriet Ziefert, M.A.
Language Arts/Reading Specialist

Ice Mice

by **Harriet Ziefert**

Illustrated by **Yukiko Kido**

flip-a

WORD

Word Families

The world is full of print. Written words are everywhere. It's impossible to learn printed words by memorizing them word, by word, by word. To make learning easier, words can be grouped into families.

The words in a word family have two or more letters that are the same. We read "ate" words and "eet" words, "et" words and "am" words. If you know "am," then it's easier to learn ram, ham, and jam.

This book has words from three different word families. All the words in a family rhyme—which means you can add other words to the group by changing the first letter.

It's okay if some of the words you think of are not *real* words. If you make "kam" or "vam" or "gam," it's not wrong— as long as you know the difference between a real word and a nonsense word.

Flip each page and presto-change-o— a new word appears!

The ice Family

m

spice

mice eat rice

spice on rice

The

unk

Family

t r

junk

junk in a trunk

skunk on a bunk

The ight Family

n

right

night light

knight at night

light on the right

knight at night with light

The ice Family

ice	rice
mice	spice
nice	twice

The unk Family

skunk	bunk
trunk	junk
clunk	sunk

The ight Family

light	knight
night	right
sight	might
height	tight

Find the words in each family.

ice light spice

rice junk bunk

trunk skunk mice

mice sight right ice

tight

skunk nice slight

dice rice bunk

clunk height spice

trunk ice light Nice

rice sunk night

mice knight

trunk sight junk right

bunk twice slice might

price bright

Word Family Activities

- Choose two words from the word family and make your own "flip-a-word" illustrations. Remember to make a cut-out at the bottom of the page where the word family shows through.

- Words in a word family rhyme. Learn a song or a poem that rhymes and share it. Or read a book that rhymes and guess which words rhyme.

- Write or tell or draw a story using two or three of the characters in this book. What happens next?